FILMED IN CORNWALL

Sue Craig and David FitzGerald

Foreword by Jenny Agutter

Bossiney Books · Launceston

First published 1999 by Bossiney Books
Langore, Launceston, Cornwall PL15 8LD
ISBN 1-899383-27-1

Front cover photograph: Clive Tickner filming Helena Bonham-Carter at Prideaux Place for a scene in *Twelfth Night*

Title page: A boat explodes off the Cornish coast (with Godrevy Lighthouse forming the backdrop) for a *Wycliffe* stunt

Acknowledgements

The authors and publishers would like to thank the many people in Cornwall and beyond who have contributed anecdotes, advice, encouragement and photographs which have made this book possible. Special thanks go to the South West Film Commission for the use of their resources.

Illustration acknowledgements
The publishers and authors gratefully acknowledge the help, co-operation and permission to reproduce photographs courtesy of the following: Mike Alsford, pages 1, 14, 15, 53 (top), 80 and 85; Alex Bailey, front cover; Boconnoc Estate, pages 46 and 47; Zed Films/Broom Parc Country House Hotel, page 78; Debbie Burdon, pages 29, 30, 31, 49 and 70; Iain Cameron, The Old Inn, pages 15 and 18; Carlton Television, pages 4, 11, 20 and 21; Henry Coleman, pages 57, 74 and 75; Henry Coleman/The Field, page 56; Sue Craig/South West Film Commission, pages 37, 71, 76, 79, 86 and 92; Duchy of Cornwall, pages 22 and 88; Diana Dunn/Portman Entertainment Ltd, page 24; Jonathan Fisher, page 61; Simon Ford/The National Trust, page 89; Mrs Ella Fraser, page 7; Granada Television Ltd, page 53 (bottom); Graham Gough, pages 38, 39, 40 and 42; H and B Graeme, Fowey, page 90; Barrie H J Hall, Braetor Studio, page 19; Annabel Hibbard/South West Film Commission, page 68; HTV/Mike Alsford, page 13; HTV/Richard Lister, page 43; LWT, page 25; Stephen F Morley/Fox Searchlight, pages 73 and 96; The National Trust, pages 33 and 44 (bottom); F B Paddy, page 6; Elisabeth Prideaux-Brune, pages 35, 50, 64, 65, 66 and 72; Renaissance Films, pages 67 and 69; Skreba Creon Films Ltd, page 59; Square Sail, page 32; John Such, pages 23 and 81; Tate Gallery, St Ives, page 12; Trewithen Estates, page 28; Twentieth Century Fox Film Corporation/Duchy of Cornwall, page 51; Paul White, page 44 (top); David Wilson, page 55. Photograph on page 63 ©1999 by Universal City Studios, Inc. Courtesy of Universal Studios Publishing Rights, a Division of Universal Studios Licensing, Inc. All rights reserved.

Printed in Great Britain by R Booth (Troutbeck Press), Mabe, Penryn, Cornwall

Contents

Cornwall, it seems, is the natural home for smouldering romance:
Tara Fitzgerald and Anthony Delon in Frenchman's Creek, *1998*

Foreword

I consider Cornwall to be my real home. It's a place to replenish energy and to enjoy the vibrant sea and sculpted rocks, brightly coloured boats jostling on the waves in coastal harbours, windswept moors, the starkness of engine house chimneys standing proud on bleak, sunset skylines, and picturesque villages vibrating to the mewing of soaring buzzards...

Cornwall is also a county of enormous industriousness. The harsh blows dealt it over the centuries have been met with courage and great resilience. Cornish people have always been able to adapt and embark on new ventures. I am proud to say that this beautiful county can now take its place among the leading film location areas of Great Britain, with a history stretching back to just before the First World War. Early records are a little sketchy, but it is thought that in 1913 Talland Bay, between Looe and Polperro, was the first place to be used for a movie. With keen support from local businesses and individuals, this was the start of what has turned out to be a long and fruitful relationship between Cornwall and the silver screen.

In *Filmed in Cornwall*, Sue Craig and David FitzGerald have done a fabulous job in shining the spotlight on casts, crews, support groups and location settings from a wonderful range of productions since the early days. Their research has thrown up amusing anecdotes, entertaining facts and figures, and unusual photographs, many snapped between scenes on or near sets. From *Doctor Who* and *Poldark* to *Twelfth Night* and *Wycliffe*, there is a rich assortment of life, drama and experience.

Living in Cornwall myself and having been involved in *The Eagle has Landed* and *A Respectable Trade*, both of which were shot here, I'm delighted to recommend a book that truly pays tribute to all who have helped put the county on the international film map.

Jenny Agutter, 1999

Local people as 'redcoats' on the set of Contraband

The early days

There is some debate as to what the first picture was to be shot in Cornwall. It is believed that a silent movie was filmed just off Talland Bay in 1913, but there is nothing surviving today to prove it. The first documented production was the 1929 silent film, *Street of Abandoned Children*, which used St Ives and Mevagissey. It starred Warwick Ward, Margaret Rawlings and the highly exotic Pola Negri. (She was probably slightly more famous for her liaisons than for her acting. Charlie Chaplin and Rudolf Valentino were among her gentlemen callers.)

However, we now know that nine years earlier in 1920 a silent film was made at Readymoney Cove, Fowey. We have received a superb photograph taken at the time, and a few memories handed down to Mr F B Paddy of Truro by his father, Edwin, who was involved in the production. Mr Paddy believes the film was called *Contraband*, but unfortunately we have found no mention of it in records. Whatever it was, we are extremely grateful to have seen this unique image of the very early days of the British film industry. It would be marvellous to think that somewhere out there a copy of *Contraband* still exists, but the chances must be very slim.

Back to 1929 and this time the shooting of *The Manxman* in Cornwall. Considering the era in which it was filmed, this is quite a racy story. It tells the tale of a Cornish fisherman who comes back to his village after he was believed drowned. He discovers that his girlfriend is now pregnant by his best friend. *The Manxman* was originally made in 1916 and was described by a critic at the time as 'of no interest, considering who the director was'. This was one of Alfred Hitchcock's first films. He went on to do a little better…

Yellow Sands *being filmed at St Leven Church in 1938*

The Phantom Light came to Port Isaac in the early 1930s, and starred Binnie Hale and a well-known singer of the time, Jack Collings. In 1933 *Forever England* with John Mills was brought to Falmouth, which had to double for the Mediterranean.

This was an era when the film industry started to bloom and, for some reason, Cornwall began to get its fair share of film productions. Within a short space of time, *Gift Horse*, starring Trevor Howard was made and then *The Man Within*, with Michael Redgrave and Richard Attenborough.

In 1938 Sennen Cove became the location for the comedy *Yellow Sands*. The story by Eden Philpotts revolves around a Cornish family's argument over a will. Starring Marie Tempest, a very young Robert Newton and character actor Wilfred Lawson, it became quite a success at the cinemas. (Legend has it that Wilfred Lawson drank Sennen dry during the filming.)

The Second World War did not stop the industry and more or less a production a year came to Cornwall until 1945. *The Thief of Baghdad* was partly shot at Gunwalloe in 1940, *Ghost Train* in Liskeard in 1941, and *Next of Kin*, with Mervyn Johns, in Mevagissey in 1942.

With the invasion of France underway, Gainsborough Films descended on the Minack Theatre, Porthcurno, in 1944 and started to work on *Love Story*. Also known as *A Lady Surrenders*, this was one of the biggest productions of its day, featuring Margaret Lockwood, Stewart Granger and Patricia Roc in the starring roles. The film was truly Cornish in all respects: the specially commissioned musical score was called 'Cornish Rhapsody' and the impressive local scenery was used to maximum effect. Even the all-star cast found it difficult to tear itself away from this magical area, staying at King Arthur's Castle Hotel at Tintagel, once a favourite haunt of Noel Coward.

As the war came to an end, there was a sudden wave of war stories throughout the film industry. *Johnny Frenchman*, shot at Mevagissey, was a tale of love, and involved a French escapee

Location shooting of the cave scenes in Miranda *was impossible: this was the model for a life-size cave which was constructed at the studio, but some location shooting was done in 1947*

making his way to Cornwall and falling for a local girl, played by Patricia Roc. With Tom Walls and Françoise Rosay, the story touches on the links between the Celtic elements of Cornwall and Brittany, and features a wrestling scene with the famous Chapman brothers, champions of the Cornish-Breton sport.

Once the war was over, the industry could now concentrate on even more productions. Gainsborough Films returned to Cornwall in 1947, bringing Glynis Johns to play the lead in *Miranda. Scott of the Antarctic* made it to Falmouth Docks in 1948, with John Mills and the quintessential Scottish gentleman James Robertson Justice.

Classic actor Sir John Mills appeared in hundreds of films and has obviously become a household name. But as an aside and little known piece of film trivia, what of James Robertson Justice – what is he best known for? Think of Lancelot Spratt, the booming irascible surgeon in *Doctor in the House* and its successors, and you have him. Many people associate him with the *Carry On* team, but although he does indeed appear in *Carry On Doctor* it is only as a portrait in a painting. The *Doctor* films were made at the same Pinewood studios as the *Carry Ons*. It is said that as a practical joke someone stuck the Lancelot Spratt picture on the wall of the *Carry On Doctor* set. It sat there behind Kenneth Williams and 'matron', without ever being noticed!

1949 saw the Walt Disney/RKO production of *Treasure Island* being made at Carrick Roads, on the rivers Fal and Helford, and at Gull Rock. Robert Newton came to Cornwall to star in this epic, but not to be outdone Patricia Roc returned for her third Cornwall-based film when she starred in *Circle of Danger* (1951) alongside Ray Milland and Marius Goring.

To touch briefly again on the *Carry On* team, the closest they ever got to Cornwall was Sussex. But many of them did take part in a 1963 film called *Crooks in Cloisters*. Filmed in and around the Portloe area, it starred amongst others Barbara Windsor and Bernard Cribbins. This motley bunch, led by Ronald Fraser, were on the run from London and took over a monastery posing as monks, monks who were turning out dodgy liquor and counterfeit money. Although the picture was shot in black and white its clarity is amazing, which may partly be because it was filmed during stunningly good weather. Bernard Cribbins remembers that it was so hot most of the monks were wandering around with shorts under their cassocks. It was also an ideal area for him to indulge in his great passion, sea fishing.

In the first fifty years of the 20th century Cornwall played an important part in the birth and support of the film industry. The films we have mentioned in brief here launched the careers of many fine actors and actresses, but more importantly they established Cornwall as a practical and powerful location setting.

Stealth among the sand dunes – Reece Dinsdale and David Threlfall in Thief Takers *at Gwithian Towans, 1996*

Watching the detectives

Over the years Cornwall has played its part in solving crimes alongside many famous detectives. A notable case was *The Return of Sherlock Holmes: The Devil's Foot*, part of a Granada series in which Jeremy Brett played the lead, supported by Edward Hardwicke, Norman Bowler and Denis Quilley. Holmes brought his magnifying glass and deerstalker to some suitably mysterious locations, including Lanyon Quoit and the Nine Maidens standing stones on the West Penwith moors. And, being in Cornwall where you can't really shoot without introducing the sea somewhere, the Lizard Peninsula, Kynance Cove, Mount's Bay and the unpretentious fishing village of Cadgwith also featured strongly.

A few years later the BBC's Inspector Alleyn travelled to Cornwall to shoot some scenes at Glebe Cliffs and the Tintagel area. Then in 1996 Cornwall was brought rapidly into the fast-paced world of the ITV series *Thief Takers*, produced by Carlton. Ironically, when they decided to film at the Tate Gallery in St Ives, there was concern at the gallery over security and extra staff were brought in for the 6 am shoot! The St Ives area and Gwithian Towans were also shown in this episode, plus the Tregenna Castle and Chy-an-Dour Hotels.

Jonathan Creek, the quirky mystery-solving drama in a genre all of its own, had a Cornish location for its first series. This series poses a real challenge for location finders, as the stories are often written around eccentric people and their equally weird homes. For one particular episode the South West Film Commission was asked for a cliff-top property. With the help of Kerrier District Council, the Commission pointed the location scout in the direction of an unusual privately-owned house perched on the cliffs at Rinsey Head.

The Tate Gallery (designed by Eldred Evans and David Shalev) at St Ives, a key location for an episode of Thief Takers, *1996*

The Wycliffe team on location at Mullion Cove

Wycliffe

The production team behind *Wycliffe* (an HTV production) use the Cornish locations, especially the coast, rather impressively. You rarely see a single episode without a shot of the boiling sea or of dramatic cliffs, and you might suspect that even if the story line does not warrant a coastline, the director will put one in anyway to make the most of the wonderful scenery.

There has been a considerable amount of press discussion about the accents in the series and the depiction of the Cornish people in general. Jack Shepherd, who plays Detective Superintendent Charles Wycliffe, and the main cast of characters do not attempt the Cornish accent. But the myriad of extras who take the roles of murderers, victims and itinerant players do.

Another case in the bag for Wycliffe...

The results, it has to be said, are not always what they might be: attempts wander from South Somerset to North Norfolk looking, we assume, for the signpost marked 'A30 Bodmin'. But casting aside, the series is a well-shot and directed drama that uses its stunning and enchanting locations to the full.

Occasionally things get a little confused, such as in the episode 'The Scapegoat' where Wycliffe suddenly turns into Wy-Clint! The suspect he is after works in a holiday theme park called Frontier City. This, for once, was the genuine name of the tourist attraction (now called The Spirit of the West) at Retallick. In the middle of a staged Wild West shoot-out, the bad guy has a gun, which of course is only a prop. He fires at the police and runs into the crowd. Wycliffe grabs a gun from one of the theme park cowboys and manages to fool our villain into thinking he is armed with a real weapon. The day is saved. But it has to be one of the strangest story lines ever written: the

All rigged up for a scene outside The Old Inn, St Breward

actor who is playing an actor with a real gun, which is actually a prop, is disarmed by an actor playing a policeman with a fake gun which the actor playing the actor is meant to think is real...

As the sun sinks slowly over the west, we will ignore the fact that the prop weapon, a double-barrelled shotgun, was fired three times without reloading, and move on to the episode 'The Number of the Beast'.

The beast to which the title refers is the infamous beast of Bodmin Moor. In the story bodies of various animals are being found and, as luck would have it, a human corpse is discovered and thought to be the victim of the big cat. Wycliffe of course manages to unravel the mystery in the standard fifty-five minutes and so ends another blood-spattered day in 'sleepy Cornwall'.

This episode was all shot in and around St Breward which for

The team – Helen Masters, Jack Shepherd and Jimmy Yuill

the purposes of the programme was renamed Tremorran. The Tremorran Arms was actually The Old Inn at St Breward, and it featured heavily in this particular episode as well as in the lives of the cast. Filming took place in one of the coldest weeks of February, brilliant sunshine but freezing. According to local gossip, every pair of thermals in Truro was bought and headed towards St Breward.

The production team moved onto the village green for two weeks and started to alter the image of the buildings to suit the script. Firstly, The Old Inn had a name change and then had to be painted a slightly dirty colour because the smart white walls were too bright. The landlord and landlady, Mr and Mrs Cameron, were quite happy and threw open their doors to the cast, crew and a dead sheep.

The sheep was in fact stuffed and was to play the slightly unchallenging role of a beast victim (not many lines and little chance of a repeat series). It had to be stored before being placed in a field ready to be filmed, so Mr Cameron suggested his garage. It was ideal. The sheep was dressed with fake blood and a large chunk of lamb was daubed on for good measure, and it was left until needed the next day.

Morning arrived, as did the cast and crew and a rather official-looking gentleman who did not seem to be part of the team. He introduced himself as the environmental health officer. There was no problem, just a routine visit, and it was suggested that the inspections started outside... in the garage where some of the freezers were kept. Unfortunately, Mr Cameron had forgotten about his fluffy, blood-soaked guest who was still lying on the floor, and as the door was opened a new *Fawlty Towers* script unfolded. Mr Cameron will always remember the expression on the health inspector's face, reminiscent of the tortured grimaces on Wycliffe's murder victims.

The Old Inn at St Breward, where Wycliffe *met* Fawlty Towers

The du Maurier mystery

Daphne du Maurier's Cornish connection has always been strong and vibrant. Her novels set in the county's varying landscapes appeal to all generations, and those that have been transferred to the cinema screen have broadened her reach still further. There is a mystery, however, surrounding the 1982 HTV filming of *Jamaica Inn*, a favourite du Maurier Cornish-based story, which at first would seem a little baffling. Here was the perfect opportunity to transform this classic tale using the correct and enchanting location as a background. But the production team chose Dartmoor, and not Cornwall.

The mystery is in fact very easily solved if you visit Jamaica Inn today. Time, tourists and the fame which the book has attracted mean that it is now totally unsuitable for portraying an early 19th-century hostelry. The A30 and modern spacious car parks built to accommodate vehicles of Daphne du Maurier fans have long since changed the face of this smuggler's haunt at Bolventor.

An exact replica of the inn was made of fibreglass and timber, and erected just outside Okehampton. It stood for over a week and was then moved to Gloucester and reassembled around another pub whose interior was used for filming.

Most people assume that Jamaica Inn stands high on cliffs overlooking a wild and threatening sea positively teeming with smugglers. In this production a group of riders leave the dark and mysterious building, gallop over a nearby tor and descend to the coast. Mysterious is the word. In a straight line, Jamaica Inn is eleven miles to Port Isaac on the north coast, the nearest handy smuggling point.

Jane Seymour played Mary Yellan, and Trevor Eve, Jem. The film also starred Billie Whitelaw and Patrick McGoohan, and was well received by the viewing public. The Cornish coastline

An exact replica of Jamaica Inn, made in 1982. It was located firstly near Okehampton, then moved to Gloucester!

at Polzeath was used as were Port Quin and Pentireglaze Haven. The fact that the main body of the picture was not shot in Cornwall raised a few eyebrows from the purists, a reaction that was to be repeated some fourteen years later with *Rebecca*.

Rebecca had actually been filmed before and did use Cornwall as a location. In the early 1970s the BBC came to Caerhays Castle and turned it into Manderley, with coastal scenes shot at Porthluney Cove. But now it was the turn of Portman Productions who were asked to produce *Rebecca* for Carlton Television in 1996. They sailed straight into hot water after deciding to film this £4 million extravaganza in the South Hams of Devon, Hampshire, Shepperton Studios and the south of France. Just one Cornish location, Charlestown, was included, but the bulk of the work went elsewhere.

Manderley, the house in *Rebecca*, is thought to have been based on du Maurier's one time Cornish home, Menabilly. But this is still occupied by the family of the original owners and was not available for filming. Du Maurier's later house, Kilmarth, where she died in 1989 at the age of 81, is also in private hands and closed to camera crews, so a house was chosen in

Charles Dance with Emilia Fox in Rebecca, *1996, walking on a South Hams beach. The 'mystery' is why Cornwall missed out...*

Hampshire, ironically the county where the story is set. Location logistics apart, Carlton Television defended itself by pointing out that the 1940 Oscar-winning Alfred Hitchcock version was shot entirely in California.

As it transpired, *Rebecca* was an incredible success, being shown in America and Europe as well as the United Kingdom and, Cornish locations or not, the county certainly benefited from the publicity it gave the area. Diana Rigg received a Primetime Emmy award for her portrayal of Mrs Danvers. Charles Dance, Emilia Fox (daughter of Edward Fox) and Faye Dunaway completed the all-star cast.

In most location decisions, logistics and cost have a large

Diana Rigg, Emilia Fox and Charles Dance at Manderley, Hants

bearing on where a film or television programme is shot. Although arguments raged in the local press that it should have been filmed in the Restormel area where du Maurier lived for most of her life, the film was so skilfully produced that the

Cornwall has plenty of ancient stones, but never in the right place! The polystyrene variety is much more amenable.
Frenchman's Creek, *filmed in 1998*

viewer, unaware of the fuss, would be none the wiser about the location.

At the time of writing this book, *Frenchman's Creek* had just been completed by Carlton Television. A watchful public and press had noted that the production used many Cornish places, including, once again, Charlestown. Filming started on 3 May 1998 with Tara Fitzgerald in the lead role. Sections of this epic were shot at Pendennis Castle and at the 16th-century Trecarrel Manor. The manor fits the mood beautifully, but the company decided the Great Hall needed a minstrels' gallery. So they built one with false doors and, as is the practice on film sets, left a security guard on night duty.

In the movie Tara Fitzgerald, who plays Dona St Columb, has

Waiting in the wings for another swashbuckling scene in
Frenchman's Creek *(on this occasion on one of Square Sail's*
boats at Charlestown)

to walk along the gallery and through the doors. But, according
to Trecarrel's owner, on one particular night Miss Fitzgerald's
place was taken by the resident ghost, and the security guard
was reduced to a gibbering wreck. Trecarrel's ghost put the
creak in Frenchman's and the fear of god into the security
guard. From that night on, the company had to position two
guards on duty, as no one wanted to be left on their own.

The story of *Frenchman's Creek* and Dona St Columb is
romance at its best. Set in the days of the Restoration, Dona
retires to her Cornish estate and falls for a French philosopher
pirate, the terror of the Cornish coast. Despite the rather quirky
storyline, the book is enchanting and the Carlton production
does it justice.

Romance blossoms at Porthgwarra, one of the locations used in Coming Home *in 1997*

Rosamunde Pilcher: Germany's TV heroine

It is not only Daphne du Maurier who has become a household name in the south west. Through the Poldark dynasty Winston Graham is another author with Cornwall in his heart who has achieved fame. But mention Cornish writer Rosamunde Pilcher and it is fans in Germany who will most rapidly fall into a state of rapturous adoration. Her popularity there is evident from the major broadcaster ZDF's viewing figures – 7-8 million for every television adaptation of her stories, including repeats (for comparison: *Wycliffe* attracts 8-10 million viewers, *Casualty*, 11-12.5 million, and *Neighbours*, 5.5-7.5 million).

Another absolutely fabulous production with Joanna Lumley, this time Coming Home

Rosamunde Pilcher has impeccable Cornish credentials. She was born in 1924 in a boarding house (Number 1, Chilecito Villas in Lelant), and lived the first years of her life at The Elms, a large Victorian semi-detached house on a hill above the Hayle Estuary. Rosamunde and sister Lalage spent their childhood playing near the beach and railway station at Lelant, occasionally catching the train which headed round the cliffs to St Ives to swim on Porthminster beach. She even met her Scottish husband on a farm called Tremedda at Zennor.

German production company Frankfurter Filmproduktion was in Cornwall for three consecutive years, from 1994 to 1996, to shoot several Pilcher stories, including *The End of Summer, Snow in April, Voices in Summer, Another View* and *The Empty*

House. They used so many genuine Cornish locations that when a different German company, UFA, approached the South West Film Commission in 1998 looking for a major country house for their adaptation of another Pilcher story, *Rosen Im Sturm*, it proved impossible to meet their brief without duplication. They finally chose a manor in East Devon.

Rosamunde Pilcher's name has become such an effective marketing tool for Cornwall that the county's tourist board have accompanied her to press conferences in Hamburg and Frankfurt. Germans with a passion for her work will have been treated on celluloid to a stroll down the cobbled streets of St Ives, a close-up view of Padstow harbour, a hike along the cliffs around Cape Cornwall followed by a drink in The Tinners Arms at Zennor. They may have paid their respects at Perranuthnoe church, enjoyed a trip to Porthminster beach, dropped by Mousehole to see if it matches its picture-postcard image, dined in gracious Prideaux Place, and rubbed shoulders with aristocracy at stately Antony House. Let's not forget Bude either, or Widemouth Bay, Mullion, Falmouth, even Penzance railway station – the list is endless. Perhaps Frankfurter were trying to rival the *Wycliffe* production team in their use of Cornish locations!

Of course, Rosamunde Pilcher also has a loyal following in the United Kingdom and other English-speaking countries. Her novel *The Shell Seekers*, which cleverly draws from her own experiences, took years to write (compared with an average of three months for most of her other stories) and reached the *New York Times* Best Seller list. It has been translated into many different languages and published in Scandinavia, Spain, Israel, Eastern Europe, Argentina, Japan and Germany. Hardly surprising then that Central TV chose to dramatise it in 1989, casting Angela Lansbury as Penelope Keeling, a woman recovering from a heart attack and seeking to relive old memories to find the answers to life's tangled web of questions.

The Shell Seekers starts by showing the distinctly honey-coloured hues of the Cotswolds, then transports us to the Mediterranean, but finally Cornwall appears and it is worth the lingering sense of anticipation which went before. St Ives is unmistakable and Porthgwarra is there for the discerning viewer to see along with Lamorna Cove and Marazion. From here on each shot seems to have been framed to show off the coastline. Occasionally an intimate conversation takes place between two actors, with a mass of granite rocks strewn in the background, and just to left of screen you get a tantalising glimpse of clotted cream-coloured sand or catch a shaft of sunlight brushing the waves, gulls swirling overhead. Then, as if the director couldn't resist that indescribable something which reminds us this really *is* Cornwall, the camera pans through 180 degrees to encapsulate the whole scene. The script says it all when Penelope tries to explain what she's been looking for, 'Something I once had and since lost – something elemental.'

Rosamunde Pilcher's mother was an honorary member of The Arts Club of St Ives and Rosamunde met many of the potters, sculptors, poets and writers who chose to settle in the town. The character Lawrence Stern, whose artistic works are a central theme in *The Shell Seekers*, was loosely modelled on Thomas Millie Dow, a local painter. Dow's house overlooked St Ives and the bay, a setting delightfully reflected in the film.

In 1997 Portman Productions and Tele-München co-produced a star-studded two-part dramatisation of *Coming Home* for ITV and ZDF respectively. It was directed by Giles Foster and the cast was like a BAFTA roll call, including Joanna Lumley, Peter O'Toole, Emily Mortimer, Penelope Keith and David McCullum. *Coming Home* was filmed on location in Cornwall for only two weeks and the team endured some of the worst summer weather of that year.

A few astute viewers realised that one of the principal locations in the story, Nancherrow, a particularly grand stately home, didn't really fit the indigenous architecture of Cornwall. Sure enough in reality it was a privately-owned aristocratic seat in Hertfordshire, while the school was a former hospital in Berkshire. However, Cornwall's Prideaux Place introduced some authenticity, this time featuring as The Dower House. And, hard as they might have tried, the producers just couldn't find a beach quite like Porthgwarra in the Home Counties.

Another location selected for *Coming Home* was a 1930s period property called Rosewyne in Church Lane, Lelant. It assumed the part of the fictional 'Windy Ridge'. For owners Terry and Yvonne Watson, it was quite an experience having their home taken over by a cast and crew of 80 plus all their equipment. But after the final day's shoot, rather than settling back into their regular domestic routine, the Watsons found the house much too quiet and followed the production to its next location in Penzance.

The sequel to *Coming Home*, *Nancherrow*, written by John Goldsmith, was put together towards the end of 1998. Once more the key locations were in the Home Counties, with a few days of second-unit photography taking place in Cornwall. Look out for flashes of Chapel Porth, Wheal Coates and Towan Head, and the Bodmin & Wenford steam railway.

Golden Manor, near Truro, used by a German film company for one of Rosamunde Pilcher's stories

Charlestown during shooting for Moll Flanders *in 1996, using the fleet of square-rigged ships which are based at the port*

The many faces of Charlestown

It goes without saying that Cornwall has a lot to offer holiday makers: spectacular coastal scenery, a fascinating mining heritage, picturesque villages, mythical castles, wild and bleak moorland. If you were to ask someone to think about Cornwall and to tell you what they saw in their mind's eye, they'd probably describe a traditional harbour, with brightly coloured fishing boats and graceful yachts bobbing on a deep blue sea, all

Onlookers and members of the cast at Charles-town in between scenes of Moll Flanders *(a Granada Television production)*

embraced by a solid grey harbour wall. Lobster pots and fishing nets are stacked on the wharf. A couple of stoic fishermen are poised beside their rods waiting for the big one. A few wizened and bewhiskered old sea dogs are engaged in that endless task of maintaining their tackle. It is a scene of tranquillity, of a county moving at its own leisurely pace.

If you expect the historic harbour at Charlestown to be like this all year round, you may be in for a bit of a surprise. If you're lucky, you might find entertainment of a completely different kind while Charlestown hosts yet another film crew.

Though the 'No waiting' cones and the huge film unit vehicles, which are all part of the production paraphernalia, may

Last minute work by the make-up team of Moll Flanders

seem a nuisance, you won't be disappointed if you stroll down to take a look at the harbourside.

During the summer months Charlestown harbour is regularly used as a film location: it becomes a hive of activity, with people scurrying around looking important, walkie-talkies in hand. Heavy electrical cables are laid to feed banks of lights which are constantly being tweaked. There may be a cherry picker (crane) on standby for an aerial shot, and a group huddled around camera, probably discussing angles or the receding light. Others may be just standing around apparently with nothing to do. But keep an eye on them when the call 'Final checks, please!' comes, for their roles in the whole fascinating process of film making should then become clearer.

The make-up assistant, shouldering a bag of goodies, adds an essential touch of powder, or realigns the principal actor's moustache. The wardrobe assistants adjust a few bodices and

Charlestown in the process of becoming Bristol Docks for
A Respectable Trade *(above and below) during filming. One of
its great advantages as a location is the possibility of constructing
sets on the long wharves with their high walls. The camera angle
can then omit the 19th-century buildings beyond*

ensure that hats are being worn at just the right rakish angle,
and the standby props people scatter some more mud and
straw on the wharf. Meanwhile the special effects team prime
the smoke-making machine.

So why is Charlestown frequently in demand as a film location? One reason in that the Grade II listed Georgian harbour
has long wharves with high walls and is particularly suited for

'dressing' as the backdrop for historical dramas. It was originally built to accommodate cargo ships which could be loaded with various commodities such as stone, pilchards, china clay, tin and copper. When they returned they brought coal, barrel staves for the local cooperages, hemp and sisal for rope-making, oak bark (a preservative), fruit, oil and limestone. The harbour has hardly changed in two hundred years and, with the addition of a few props – wagons, barrels of rum, smouldering braziers – the wharf soon becomes an old trading port once again.

From the harbour entrance there is a clear view out to the open sea, with only the occasional freighter to worry about in the distance. With the use of the hydraulic lock gate, which can be dropped to allow boats access, water levels can be controlled. Added to this, the harbour walls are ideal for building film sets and, over the years, Charlestown has been transformed by imaginative production designers to portray wartime Alderney in the Channel Islands for *The Eagle has Landed*, 18th-century Bristol docks for the slave-trade drama *A Respectable Trade*,

Phoenix *performs for* Moll Flanders *at Turnaware Point in 1996*

Chatham docks for *Moll Flanders*, Hamburg for *Amy Foster*, Polruan for *Frenchman's Creek* and, most recently, Portsmouth for the feature film *Mansfield Park*. It has also provided backdrops for *Poldark* and *The Onedin Line*.

But the crowning glory at Charlestown, and part of the package which now attracts film makers from all over the world, is the fleet of square-rigged boats belonging to Square Sail, a company originally set up in 1978 in Colchester, Essex, by Robin Davies. (He moved to Cornwall 15 years later.)

Whenever you visit, you may be treated to the sight of one of these magnificent boats moored alongside. They are as versatile as the harbour itself: *Phoenix* was Christopher Columbus's vessel *Santa Maria* for *1492: Conquest of Paradise*, and in *Frenchman's Creek* she became *La Mouette*, a two-masted brig, while *Aurora* was transformed from *The Rose* in *A Respectable Trade* to *Earl of Pembroke* in *Frenchman's Creek*. And sometimes the change literally happens overnight, such as when *La Mouette* became *Daydream* for a one-day *Scarlet Pimpernel* shoot.

Charlestown can look absolutely enchanting. When the beacons were burning at the harbour entrance on a clear summer night in 1998 for the filming of *Frenchman's Creek*, *Phoenix* glided out into the sea and there was really no need for the usual request, 'Quiet, please', to cast, crew and onlookers. A reverent silence had descended on everyone who had endured the long hours of waiting for this particular scene. For a moment, you could block out the artificial lighting, the scattered crew anticipating the end of a long day, and the group around the camera. Charlestown wasn't a film set at all: it was a pretty Cornish harbour slipping into another historical role with the easy grace of a professional.

A private omnibus, as used by Victorian hotels to bring guests from the station, here making an appearance in Twelfth Night

Transport old and new

For a short while in the 1980s nearly every British Rail advert seemed to have a shot of the Brunel railway bridge at Saltash, with Jimmy Saville or some other voice-over extolling the virtues of a rail system that barely served the county it was filmed in. Trains, however, have always played a large part in Cornwall, and over the years have appeared both on film and television.

The railway at St Erth featured in a 1982 BBC television adaptation of Virginia Woolf's *To the Lighthouse*. But way before that Glynis Johns can be seen stepping out of a train at the old Fowey station in 1947 for the film *Miranda*. So many of the old Cornish branch lines are now just ghostly memories, although one favourite film, *Ghost Train*, vividly brings back some real images, ideal for the spotter of ancient trains.

The phantom first popped up in 1927 as a silent movie and then again in 1931. In 1943 it was manifested screaming through the Devon countryside, over the Tamar rail bridge and on into Cornwall. The play on which the film was based was set entirely in Cornwall and was written by Arnold Ridley (most famous for playing Godfrey in *Dad's Army*). In the 1943 movie Liskeard station was one of the locations, and actual footage of the GWR line through Devon and Cornwall blended in with studio scenes.

The stars of the last production of *Ghost Train* came from the golden age of cinema and, like Arnold Ridley, have now passed away. Arthur Askey took the lead role and by his side, towering above him, was his playmate Richard Murdoch. Ignoring the story line, it is a perfect opportunity to catch a glimpse of the old steam rail system that formed the main artery through Cornwall.

From trains to planes. Cornwall should have been shown in one of the world's most famous movies by James Stewart, but sadly it was not. In *The Spirit of St Louis*, Stewart, playing Charles Lindbergh, dips his plane wing and looks out of the cockpit window as he is nearing the end of his epic trans-Atlantic flight. According to the film, he spots Plymouth (then in Devon), depicted as two green fields, a church spire and a few houses. But in real life the direction Lindbergh was looking in was towards Tideford (Cornwall), which was indeed two green fields, a church spire and a few houses.

Lindbergh is said to have flown over Tideford, and one or two of the old local farmers still remember the unusual sight of an aircraft overhead as presumably 'The Spirit of St Louis' passed by and out to sea again. But whether Lindbergh, history or the script writers got it wrong, is a mystery. What can be said is that Tideford can hold its head high and assert it *should* have been up there, named, on the silver screen.

And so from planes to coaches. In 1967 the Beatles decided

to make *Magical Mystery Tour*, and they chose the south west for filming. After causing chaos in Devon, their coach becoming wedged on a bridge near Widecombe and causing the biggest traffic jam Dartmoor has ever seen, they went on to Cornwall. The fab four stayed at The Atlantic Hotel in Newquay, using various locations in and around the area, including Towan Beach and Bodmin. But the film was panned by the critics and, as Brian Epstein their manager had just committed suicide, 1967 turned out to be more miserable for them than magical.

The late Willie Rushton and crew filming at the Launceston Steam Railway in 1996. Cameramen get used to working in precarious positions – fixed or, in this case, moving

Actor Christopher Biggins (Reverend Osborne Whitworth) talking to Poldark *author Winston Graham during a break in shooting*

(All the Poldark *photographs reproduced here were taken by Graham Gough.)*

Poldark and the Boconnoc connection

Just outside Lostwithiel stands one of the largest private working estates in Cornwall. Boconnoc was once the property of the Pitt family, bought by Thomas Pitt in 1713 and subsequently becoming the retreat of William Pitt the younger. It is currently owned by the Fortescue family who have maintained and managed this superb 8000 acre estate which spreads out around the house.

It offers a wealth of film location opportunities, mainly because of the care and attention the present owners have devoted to its upkeep. To date, millions of viewers have already seen this beautiful part of Cornwall on television and in the cinema. *Poldark* (and later *The Three Musketeers*), set against

Filming at St Winnow's church. Above: Christopher Biggins and Ralph Bates being 'tracked'. Below: Robin Ellis talks to the crew

Robin Ellis, Angharad Rees, Judy Geeson and Michael Cadman
during filming of the famous wedding scene in the second series

the elegant backdrop of Boconnoc, created an enormous impact when it first hit television screens in the autumn of 1975. The BBC had no idea quite what a success they had on their hands. At its peak, it attracted an audience of 15 million viewers and went on to be sold in forty-five countries. Today it still has a dedicated following, easily proven by hitching up to the Internet and searching the word 'Poldark'. The home page is constantly changing with comments and questions from fans around the world. Ask anyone over the age of twenty-five to name a Cornish-based television series, and ninety per cent will say *Poldark*. Even *Wycliffe* or the du Maurier dramas must walk in the shadow of this true giant among Cornish productions.

Before mentioning the part Boconnoc played, we can take you on a swift visit to some of the other historic houses and locations that were used in the production – although it would be easier to say where *Poldark* wasn't filmed!

Ross Poldark and his immediate family went through more houses than woodworm and to follow their exact moves is a little complicated. To start with, Ross inherited 'Nampara', which in the novels stands above 'Nampara Cove'. For filming purposes the cove was in fact a selection of inlets and cliffs between Pendeen and Levant, and in the first series alone, Nampara was actually two separate houses – Pendeen Manor Farm and Botallack Manor Farm. For series two, the exterior of a 17th-century manor and farm were used near Port Quin. These buildings were well known to the author, Winston Graham, who at one time lived in Perranporth and partly based the interior of Nampara on the manor.

Francis and Elizabeth Poldark lived at 'Trenwith', later to become the home of George Warleggan and Elizabeth when she remarried. In the first series Trenwith was Godolphin Hall near Helston, but magically became Trerice Manor, the National Trust property near Newquay, in the second. If you were reading the books and following the series, you might have been slightly confused by now, but it was about to get worse. Enter Boconnoc or Aunt Agatha's estate of 'Penrice'. Trenwith had burnt to the ground and Elizabeth, now married to George, moved in with Aunty (who never appeared in the first series, but who became vital in the second).

With Boconnoc as the central location, the second series saw much work in and around Lostwithiel – the famous wedding of Dwight Enys and Caroline Penvenen was shot at St Winnow's Church. Judy Geeson played Caroline and Michael Cadman, Dwight (Richard Morant took the part of Dwight in the first series).

The familiar figure of Christopher Biggins starred as the Reverend Osborne Whitworth, while the intrusive shape of the Fowey to Lostwithiel train also tried to get in on the act. On

Poldark v. Warleggan at cricket must have been the best attended charity match ever played in Cornwall, with a crowd estimated at more than 6000 over-running the ground at Boconnoc. To the relief of the fans, Poldark won!

more than one occasion production had to be halted as it made its way into the background.

Perhaps one of the greatest indications of the popularity of *Poldark* was the attendance at a charity cricket match between the Poldark XI and the Warleggan XI. It was played on a pitch at Boconnoc, and everyone assumed that if the weather stayed fine a couple of hundred dedicated fans would make their way there and cheer on good against evil. In the event, the police had to open all the gates to the estate to relieve the build-up of cars on the main roads. No one is sure how many people saw the Poldark victory, but estimates are in excess of six thousand.

Robin Ellis will always be Ross Poldark and, to millions of people, *Poldark* will always be Cornwall. And the beautiful actress Angharad Rees will for ever be Demelza, a name Winston Graham took from a signpost on Goss Moor.

If you carry on towards Liskeard, you will see the sign for Warleggan. The evil George Warleggan was played superbly by Ralph Bates, in reality a man totally unlike his character. Kind and thoughtful, he was always ready to greet the hundreds of fans who followed the filming. Sadly, he is no longer with us, but his memory and that of a truly Cornish series live on.

It is said that the only thing which can possibly spoil a great memory is 'to return', and there's no doubt some truth in this. Ten years after *Poldark*, there were letters of protest, legal action and picketing. And that was before the programme in question went on air. This was not some highly controversial World in Action documentary, but the 1995 HTV production of a new 'Poldark', *Poldark –The Stranger from the Sea*.

Mel Martin as Demelza and John Bowe as Ross Poldark in the much maligned Poldark – The Stranger from the Sea

Sometimes location shots can give an idea of how Cornwall used to look. Here is Wheal Prosper as it now is (above) and (below) as it looked dressed for Poldark – The Stranger from the Sea

It is difficult to know where to start when talking about this saga. Although our book is about locations, we must admit very little is known about where it was filmed. All we can verify is that it was shot in and around Cornwall, and that the exact sites were kept secret, as there had already been a well-orchestrated protest campaign in the press against its filming and a demonstration by fans of the original series, some in period dress, at HTV headquarters. The Poldark die-hards were not happy that Robin Ellis and Angharad Rees had been dropped from this remake. In fact, it was reported that Miss Rees even started legal action, which was later dropped. Robin Ellis also had a few things to say on the subject of casting. Journalists disclosed that he was approached by HTV and took part in lengthy discussions about the filming, but then there was a sudden change of heart.

The 5000 strong Cornwall-based Poldark Appreciation Society rose as one. A delegation managed to meet with an executive producer who offered a Teletext page on ITV so that viewers could register their opinions. Letters began to pour into local and national papers.

Television chiefs had set a target that the £1.5 million programme should reach ten million viewers. When 'P'-day finally arrived, it managed a healthy nine million in early indications. John Bowe played Ross and Mel Martin, Demelza, and the end result reflected excellent filming and acting, with precise period detail. Love it or loathe it, it received more publicity than any other programme at the time.

The BBC videos of the original series are still one of the all-time best sellers. The web site pages continue to mirror the interest in the 1970s production, but as for *The Stranger from the Sea*, he appears to have left his clothes on the beach and done a Reggie Perrin.

Back to Boconnoc and this time *The Three Musketeers*. When the author Alexander Dumas died, he was nearly bankrupt.

Setting the scene around a specially-constructed bridge at Boconnoc for the Musketeers to swash their buckles

Today he would be a multi-millionaire, as his story has been made into dozens of films, television programmes and even cartoons. Every two or three years another version hits the streets, with more or less the same plot, but it's one the public loves again and again.

In 1993 Walt Disney ventured forth with flashing blade and swirling cape, using Lanhydrock, Charlestown, Pentire and Boconnoc as locations. Keifer Sutherland played Athos, Charlie Sheen, Aramis, and Oliver Platt, Porthos. Chris O'Donnell took the part of D'Artagnan and the impressive Tim Curry was the evil Cardinal Richelieu. Boconnoc and the surrounding estate were transformed into Versailles and 18th-century France.

Heavy wooden bridges were built, minor modern day fixtures were covered up, the fancy fortifications of Versailles' roof line were constructed at ground level, and hedges with fake foliage were added. The attention to detail was incredible, with the pictured carriages looking as if they had just been hauled by sweating teams of four horses on the rough road to Paris ahead of the Cardinal's men. In truth there was a small electric motor under the back axle and they were closer to Penzance than to Paris. The film was a great success and, as swashbuckling goes, it reached 8 on the Richter scale...or should that be the Richelieu scale?

The stableyard at Boconnoc takes on a French appearance

Commercial break

Now let's take a short break. Commercial making is one of the most prolific industries in the world of television production, and literally hundreds of advertisements are put together each year. Star-studded and sometimes more entertaining than the programmes they intersect, these big budget extravaganzas can provide enormous scope to mislead, especially where locations are concerned.

Some years ago the Rover 213 was launched with an advert shot in the south west. The car is seen gliding over Bodmin Moor and turning down a leafy lane in the South Hams. It slides past Yealmpton, Bigbury and Hope Cove. A 1300cc engine, it would seem, has just managed to propel a vehicle thirty miles in thirty seconds.

Shell Oil used part of the north Cornwall coast and a host of other shots to film one of their commercials. The highly complicated advert with cleverly computer-edited sections contains a man walking along a road, then riding on a push bike, travelling on a train, and then in a boat through a bunch of catamarans, and finally over a bank, into a gymkhana and on up to cliffs surrounded by hang gliders.

The theme is something along the lines of 'Shell gets you there!' The tiny problem was that they were shooting the gymkhana scene near the tree-lined river Dart in Devon and the hang glider part on the north Cornwall coast where there were no trees. For continuity's sake they obviously needed trees. Solution: dig one up and plant it on the cliff.

Unfortunately, the weather deteriorated and the filming was delayed. After a while things picked up and the crew returned to a now rather brown tree. Solution: spray it green. Simple really and that is what they did, confusing a few people in the process. There are very few trees on the north Cornwall coast;

Tombstone Pizza used the old Tehidy Hospital as a French chateau – 'Tis a far better pizza that I do now??

even fewer have a couple of coats of paint on them to freshen them up.

Hot delicious pizza from the heart of pizza country where the locals know how to make the traditional dish, just as they have done for generations in...Camborne. Yes, Camborne was chosen as a location for a French Revolution style commercial selling pizza! Quite why an Italian product with American associations should be shot in Cornwall using a French story line is a little strange, but it does prove that the world truly is a global village.

The services of The Royal Hotel in Truro were brought into play when the company making the advertisement arrived. The Royal were asked to store five thousand pizzas, and they duly obliged. As for the supposed French chateau, it was in fact Tehidy Hospital, now closed and redeveloped as private houses. Whether the commercial was a success or not, we are not sure, but we can't help wondering what happened to the five thousand pizzas. At the time of writing, you can still buy one or two of the new houses at Tehidy. Should you be tempted, it might

Prideaux Place played host to a cantankerous IBM monkey

be worth checking what the insulation is made from.

Finally in this break, we must mention IBM, the computer company which selected Prideaux Place for one of its commercials. First rule of television is: never work with children or animals. IBM wanted a monkey to type on a keyboard in the library of this magnificent house, but it was obviously not computer-literate, became bored, threw a bit of a wobbler and ran up the shelves. At the top of the bookcase, it relieved itself, much to the chagrin of the producer. Eventually, after much commotion and hair-pulling (of the non-monkey variety) the set was cleared and order restored.

Making commercials is a very strange pastime and the examples mentioned here may seem bizarre and totally unorthodox. Most advertisements have huge budgets and it is not uncommon for very successful writers and directors to be employed on these thirty-second cameos. Large teams of professionals are brought together briefly and then disbanded after the work is done. Again, cost is all-important, and easy access to facilities is vital, something which Cornwall has provided time and time again for the industry.

Relatively safe to work with – a moulded narwhal for When the Whales Came, *filmed on Scilly; notice his tusk following behind!*

'Never work with animals...'

Some creatures will do anything to get in on the act, even if it's for a posthumous credit. During the filming of *Twelfth Night* at Prideaux Place, the crows which hung out in the trees surrounding the house were being particularly raucous, venting their disapproval of proceedings with a cacophony of caws. The row was seriously disrupting filming, so the owners decided to post a man in the grounds, armed with a shotgun which he discharged periodically. Unfortunately a pigeon, not even responsible for the racket, just happened to be on the wrong flight path at the wrong time. It collided with a fatal amount of shot, and hurtled to the ground, landing unceremoniously in a very dead heap at Mel Smith's feet.

From pigeons to donkeys. Margaret-Joyce, a donkey described by her owner Claire Belton as 'an ageing character actress', was selected for a walk-on part in the feature film *Oscar and Lucinda*. Claire runs a donkey sanctuary and animal extras agency at St Kew. It was a chance in a million to act (or rather act up) opposite stars Ralph Fiennes and Cate Blanchett. For the luckless Margaret-Joyce, her role as the fish wife's donkey meant standing right at the end of Boscastle Harbour, something she wasn't too keen on doing because she was very nervous of water. She eventually calmed down during the rehearsals, but her nerves returned whenever the words 'Turn over' were called. Her automatic response was to try to throw her handler, the other extras, and any crew who happened to be close enough, into the harbour. Needless to say, the Margaret-Joyce action movie scenes ended up on the cutting room floor – her antics were not quite in keeping with the story line of *Oscar and Lucinda*, even though the film is about 'a magnificently flawed, laudanum swigging 19th-century cleric'.

And for Ratcatcher, a trusty steed more accustomed to flying around the countryside with the North Cornwall Hunt than working as a stunt horse, the opportunity for a moment of glory came in *Omen III: The Final Conflict*. When the leading actor's horse, a temperamental thoroughbred, refused to co-operate and go over a ramp especially constructed for the shot at Roche Rock, 'Rattie', a bold and reliable hunter was chosen as the stand-in. Sadly for Rattie, though, he couldn't star as himself and had to be painted to match the other horse.

Perhaps the best-known Cornish equine advertising star was Beeatus, the beautiful black horse used by Lloyds Bank. The image of this magnificent animal charging through the surf caught the imagination of many television viewers and Beeatus became a celebrity. He was stabled near St Breward, and the beach advert was shot on Pentewan Sands. Sadly he recently passed away at the age of twenty-two.

Not everyone looks quite equally at home on a horse... We shall name no names! (*Above:* Poldark, 1995; *below:* Moll Flanders)

For children, *Little Pig Robinson* was one of those films that blended superb animal costumes with real life. Polperro and the surrounding area was picked as a backdrop. You can see many strange and wonderful things in Polperro, and in 1990 this would have included a two-metre tall goose selling cockles and mussels. It's probably best to watch the film rather than for us to try to explain it. If you or your children do, keep an eye out for a few little errors: a motorboat, a diver's shoulder and a motor home on the cliffs at Talland Bay all creep into the picture at some point!

And so to *Wind in the Willows*, a book that has a close association with Cornwall. Kenneth Graham was married and spent a great deal of his life in Fowey. When he wrote the story, he could not have conceived just how successful and popular his work would become. Films, cartoons, other books and stage plays have all emanated from this classic. The media has even looked at the life of Graham, with the BBC returning to Fowey for a drama documentary.

In 1995 the Camel estuary was one of the locations chosen for a film of *Wind in the Willows*, directed by Terry Jones of *Monty Python* fame. With wonderful evil weasels, Steve Coogan as Mole, fellow Python Eric Idle as Ratty, Nicol Williamson as Badger, and Terry playing the part of Toad as well, it was one of the finest versions of the story yet made. Kenneth Graham would surely have been hugely delighted with it. The end result on screen was an enchanting tale, told beautifully and reflecting an age of innocence that seems long past. If you're a *Wind in the Willows* fan, you can see the original text written by Graham in The Greenbank Hotel in Falmouth.

Short and ... sweet?

A request for assorted rare breeds – chickens, sheep, cows and some blackbirds – formed part of one of the more unusual enquiries received by the South West Film Commission in 1996. Henry Coleman, the writer, director and producer of *Pigment*, a short but charming surreal comedy which looks at life through the eyes of Salvador Dali, was absolutely serious. What's more, he was determined to shoot in Cornwall. As with most young film makers, he was working on a shoestring and his bizarre location brief caused a few raised eyebrows.

He asked, 'Can you help us find a field in bloom, a gothic-style house, and a tree next to a path? By the way, the tree will have to be big enough to hold five jazz musicians who will turn into blackbirds!' He also needed a couple of skilled fencers (of the sword-brandishing variety) for a scene in the sand dunes. With very little in the way of location budgets, Henry somehow persuaded people in Cornwall to help with his project.

He found a golden meadow, woodland with an ancient tree

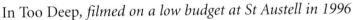

In Too Deep, *filmed on a low budget at St Austell in 1996*

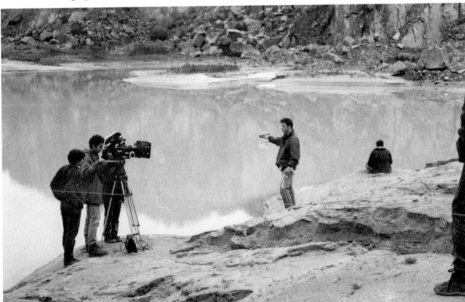

A film about Salvador Dali might reasonably be expected to be bizarre…

suitable for his musicians, rippling streams, a field of cows and a beach bathed in sunshine looking more like the Caribbean than England. With some imaginative graphics, he turned a fairly ordinary house into something unusual enough to pass as Dali's studio. Tim Potter, who looks remarkably like John Cleese, brought wit and sensitivity to the role of Salvador Dali, and the film, which was shot at Lamorna Cove, Porthmeor Cove and Gwithian Towans, received a special screening in St Ives.

Another short film, *In Too Deep*, in which two ordinary people are thrown into a solemn tale of love and tragedy, is a bleak thriller set in and around St Austell. Originally called *The Pit*, it was filmed in the St Austell clay pits in 1996. Students from the local College Media Centre volunteered to work on this production as general dogsbodies.

Within their duties of coffee making, location scouting and driving, they were asked to find a suitable looking corpse. They tried the leisure centre for life-saving dummies, but these were deemed too butch for the role, so an alternative was eventually devised – a boiler suit stuffed with plastic bags.

The clay pits have other claims to fame, including being used as a distant planet in a *Dr Who* adventure. In the 1970s the Doctor and the TARDIS travelled through time in Cornwall, narrowly missing the crew of *Blake's Seven* who also popped in for a little filming. And talking of *Dr Who*, here are some more film trivia. Would you be surprised to hear that Beryl Reid played in an episode, as did Jason Connery, Leslie Grantham and John Cleese? And having mentioned John Cleese we might as well reveal that most of the Python team have filmed in Cornwall over the years, some with independent productions. In the early 1980s Cape Cornwall was used as the location for a *Ripping Yarns* story called 'Whinfrey's Last Case' with Michael Palin.

... but a tree holding five jazzmen who turn into blackbirds?

Sun, sea and surf dudes – Cornish style

Who says surfing movies can't be created in the UK? *Blue Juice* made a brave attempt to prove that whatever can be done in the United States, the British can do just as...well, why don't you watch it and decide for yourself?

Never mind the fact that the ultimate 'tube', the really big wave, is shot in Lanzarote; the beaches and rollers around Newquay still look impressive.

Shades are an essential prop in this film, worn religiously by the cool guys – JC, Josh and Dean – and distinctly lacking in the plump, about-to-be-married, non-surfing Terry. However, *Blue Juice* is not so much about 'being in the line up', surfing 'the tube', achieving a 'hang ten' or regularly 'wiping out'. It's a romantic comedy that attempts to combine an observation of surfing culture with the more serious themes of finding potential and seeking fulfilment.

For JC (Sean Pertwee) the big 'three O' is just around the corner, and he wants to surf his way around the world before it's too late. But he's torn between the demands of his gorgeous girlfriend Chloe (Catherine Zeta Jones) and his passion for the sea. Chloe runs the Aqua Shack, a café popular with the surf dudes, but rather peculiarly situated on the quay at Mousehole. When she's not working, she likes to develop her culinary skills in the bedroom. JC dons his pinafore with little resistance when desired by Chloe, much to the amusement of his younger mates, but he still can't resist the call of the surf.

So the story unfolds, interlinked by the appalling 'ooh-aarhh' Cornish accents on 'Smuggler FM' local radio. The surf dudes of Newquay are gradually exposed as a bunch of losers with hang-ups. JC isn't getting any younger and he still hasn't taken up the final challenge to surf the 'Boneyard'. Josh (Steven Macintosh) has lost his musical soul. Terry (Peter Gunn) is a

The cast of Blue Juice *at Newquay – it's more a romantic comedy than a 'surf movie'*

couch potato, living his life through the television screen. And Dean (Ewan McGregor) is all tied up in drugs and underhand deals. Cornwall is unflatteringly summed up as 'this godforsaken, disease-ridden dump', and to cap it all the Aqua Shack is going to be auctioned. Thankfully, by the end of the film things have improved for all concerned and Cornwall shrugs off its miserable image to become part of a generally happy ending.

Chapel Porth, Trevellas Coombe and the Blue Hills Valley work well as the suitably grim 'Boneyard'. The streets of St Ives and the beaches around Newquay and Godrevy interwoven with shots of awesome waves crashing on unforgiving rocks also speak of Cornwall, even if some of the footage came from the Canary Isles.

Terror on the dark side

A number of chilling, scary films have materialised on Cornwall's shores. Some characters have come in search of blood, others have left with the devil, but all have instilled terror...

But this terror is dissipated somewhat when, for example, you recognise Jericho Valley and the Blue Hills near St Agnes in the 1971 film *Crucible of Terror*. Dracula's castle seems strangely familiar in the 1970s version of *Dracula* for BBC television with Louis Jordan and Susan Penhaligan. Could the lair of the Prince of Darkness actually be St Michael's Mount? And was that a bat flapping across Carlyon Bay and Mevagissey?

Just when you thought it was safe to go out once more in an open-neck shirt, old bat-features materialises again in 1978 to hang around St Michael's Mount and King Arthur's Castle Hotel. Universal Pictures put together an all-star cast of Frank Legella, Kate Nelligan, Trevor Eve, Donald Pleasance and Sir Lawrence Olivier. The actors, the setting and the work that was put into the production ensured it became a classic 'Dracula'.

For true terror, perhaps, there is 1981's *Omen III: The Final Conflict* starring Sam Neill as Damien Thorn. Damien is the Ambassador to the Court of St James and head of a multi-national company. The world is gripped with recession and uncertainty as he moves from strength to strength, spreading disaster while he heads for the top job, the presidency.

One part of the film requires a full hunt, hounds and a sizeable hunting field. Prideau House and the Luxulyan viaduct area were used as locations, while the North Cornwall Hunt provided their services. Numerous foxes were supplied for filming, and later released. We can only guess how the production team came across a plentiful supply, but there was a scurrilous rumour that they bought the same animal on several occasions.

We'll draw a discreet veil over that one, but at the end of the

Simon Hunter, its director, described Lighthouse *as 'a dark brooding nightmare, a descent into hell'*

shooting, which took three or four days, there were more foxes running around than you could shake a big stick at. On one particular occasion when 'Action' was called, the hunt rode off only to come across a fox that had been set free earlier. Off took the hounds in full cry, with horses and riders in hot pursuit. After half an hour normality returned, but the continuity of the film had gone to the dogs as the horses were now sweating and covered in mud. The film crew had broken their golden rule of never working with children ... or foxes.

If you've seen *Omen III* and thought it was frightening, that was nothing compared with the critics' reviews, although politeness and good manners stop us from mentioning even some of the better reports. If you should sit through this white knuckle ride of mediocrity again, or for the first time, watch out for some minor role players and you may recognise a few familiar faces. Ruby Wax plays the secretary to the American Ambassador, and Eric Richard (Sergeant Cryer from *The Bill*) is an astronomer's assistant.

While on the subject of terror, *Straw Dogs* from 1971 ought to be mentioned. If you haven't seen it, it's the tale of a peace-loving American who moves his wife to an isolated village where he is constantly harassed and his wife attacked. The result: violence...a lot of it. This Sam Peckinpah movie has always conjured up high emotions: some say it is a classic of its time, a wonderful study of human response to excessive brutal-ity; others call it degrading and pointless, and bracket it with *Clockwork Orange* and *Last Tango in Paris*. It was filmed at St Buryan and Lamorna Cove, and starred Dustin Hoffman and Susan George, with Peter Vaughan (who was the 'genial' Harry Grout in *Porridge*). Let's just say it's not a film for all tastes.

Moving on to *Lighthouse* Simon Hunter, its director, described it as 'a dark brooding nightmare...a descent into hell'. It's more of a thriller than a horror story, centring around the gruesome and malevolent activities of a mass murderer, Leo Rook, played by Chris Adamson who became something of a cult figure for his portrayal of Mean Machine in *Judge Dredd*. He escapes from a prison ship which has been struggling in tempestuous seas and makes his way to the nearby Gehenna Lighthouse, kills the lighthouse keepers and disables the beam.

When the prison ship *Hyperion* finally loses her struggle with the elements, smashing into Gehenna Rocks, a few survivors including the doctor played by Rachel Shelley and prisoner Richard Spader (James Purefoy), who's been sentenced for manslaughter, manage to reach the lighthouse. Here their numbers are systematically depleted as they come face to face with 'the most feared man in Europe', a ruthless killer who likes to stalk his victims when they are alone...

Lighthouse took four years to develop and is the first feature project for Hunter and producer Mark Leake. It is a relatively low-budget movie that combines traditional model-based tech-niques and hi-tech computer-generated special effects. So,

King Arthur's Castle Hotel sprouted a graveyard in Dracula, *1979*

where do locations fit into the equation? The rocks on which *Hyperion* founders are largely modelled on those at the base of Longships Lighthouse off Land's End. Longships itself also provided inspiration for the two scale models of the lighthouse used at Three Mills Island Studios where principal photography took place during the summer of 1998. The second-unit photography crew went to Land's End to get authentic shots of the sea and rocks. And the prison ship *Hyperion* is played by none other than the Isles of Scilly Steamship Company's cargo boat *Gry Maritha*.

Hunter says *Lighthouse* is not a 'blood and guts' horror film. Yes, it will appeal to people who like to be frightened, but the fear lies in creating an atmosphere of nerve-wracking suspense. The rest lies in the viewer's own imagination. For those of us fascinated by Cornish locations, part of the intrigue will lie in distinguishing the real thing from the special effects – that's if we can bear to open our eyes.

*The drawing room
redesigned for*
Twelfth Night

Prideaux Place gets a face lift

Prideaux Place is a gracious and serene house which gives the impression of being isolated, while it is actually situated right on the edge of Padstow. If you stand outside the front door to this Elizabethan manor, the rolling parkland and estuary unfold before your eyes. But if you take a stroll around the deer park, you can see that the older part of the town is adjacent to the grounds, and twentieth-century development sprawls within view.

The shell grotto constructed especially for Twelfth Night

The original Prideaux Place was built by Sir Nicholas Prideaux in the 1530s, and has been in the same family ever since. As a film location it has much to offer, with eighty-one rooms in total, forty-four being bedrooms. During the Second World War, it was used as a base for American army personnel. Many of the rooms they occupied have remained untouched, although one of them became Ralph Fiennes' particularly austere bedroom recently for the Australian production of *Oscar and Lucinda*. It didn't need much in the way of dressing!

Peter and Elisabeth Prideaux-Brune, who live in the house today, are accustomed to the idiosyncrasies of film crews. Prideaux has served as a location for two Rosamunde Pilcher stories: *The End of Summer*, for German company Frankfurter Filmproduktion, and *Coming Home* for Portman, plus commercials and the occasional stills shoot. As it is open to the public during the summer, filming at this time must be dovetailed

Allowing a film company into your home can involve an immense amount of disruption, and they expect to be allowed to do whatever is in the best interests of the film. Even by the usual standards, the work done at Prideaux Place for Twelfth Night *was exceptionally far-reaching*

around visitors. With so many rooms available, smaller projects can almost go unnoticed, but occasionally the public and participants in a production bump into each other.

For the IBM commercial mentioned on page 50, the supporting role was played by a man clad head to toe in armour. He didn't actually do or say anything, but just stood around or, between takes, wandered through the house in his costume. At the same time as this particular shoot, Prideaux Place was also hosting a group of genteel ladies for a guided tour. They were unaware of the advert being filmed, but kept encountering a rather animated suit of armour, certainly one that was occupied. The atmosphere of this historic house took on a much different meaning for them, and some had a real 'touch of the vapours'.

Production company Renaissance were looking for a distinctly Celtic location for their feature film *Twelfth Night*. They had originally considered Ireland for the fictional Illyria, but could not find the right property to reflect the pre-Raphaelite/Victorian look desired by director Trevor Nunn. When Nunn saw Prideaux Place, he knew straight away that this was the right location for his production, and other places in the county were ideally suited to his vision, offering everything according to him 'from the formal prose of gracious gardens to the high drama of its coastal landscape'.

Prideaux and The National Trust's Lanhydrock impressed Nunn and designer Sophie Becher. They were solid grey stately homes, remote, majestic and somewhat isolated by their huge dreamy gardens. The interiors were luxurious but not ostentatious, giving the impression of wealth while remaining comfortable and, as far as Sophie was concerned, Cornwall had just the right fairy tale quality they were seeking.

Imogen Stubbs and Richard E Grant brandish swords in the orchard; Peter Gunn and Mel Smith ensure rules are observed

Nigel Hawthorne as Malvolio in Twelfth Night, *filmed at Prideaux Place*

Prideaux underwent a major face lift for *Twelfth Night*, with the owners allowing the production designer and art department virtually free rein. The attention to detail was nothing short of extraordinary. The floor in the main hall was first stripped bare, then painted in an ornate Italianate style. An extra stained-glass window was painted in a staircase hallway and all the woodwork was grained for Victorian authenticity.

The drawing room was decorated in grandiose style, with a specially designed mural running around the walls. The first attempt at the mural was rejected and whitewashed over. All that work for nothing! Second time around, painted by scenic artist Steven Sallybanks and incorporating a romantic view of St Michael's Mount, it was accepted. Then the final touches were added – drapes, furniture and props. The drawing room,

Lanhydrock was another Cornish location used for Twelfth Night. *Here is Helena Bonham-Carter with Steven Mackintosh*

with its moody lighting and sumptuous furnishings, perfectly complemented actress Helena Bonham-Carter's portrayal of the tragic Olivia, in mourning for a self-imposed period of seven years following the deaths of her father and brother.

Arguably, the *pièce de résistance* for *Twelfth Night* at Prideaux Place was one of the least expensive in terms of materials. Renaissance Production's art department created an intricate ornamental grotto containing thousands of shells coming from nearby beaches, local fishermen and Rick Stein's restaurant in Padstow. It formed part of the Italianate garden, providing a stunning backdrop for Malvolio (Nigel Hawthorne) as he mistakenly interprets a fraudulent love letter while Sir Toby Belch (Mel Smith), Sir Andrew Aguecheek (Richard E Grant) and Fabian (Peter Gunn) smirk and wriggle, dart and squirm behind the topiary garden – also imported for the production.

The weather and other unpredictables

Filming in Cornwall can be fraught with hazards – unpredictable weather and animals, occasionally unco-operative extras, tides turning at the wrong time, and dedicated hikers determined to walk the coast path just as the shot has been set up for that crucial scene on the cliffs in a costume drama. But perhaps the most frustrating thing for film crews is that of ineffective mobile phones.

It seems that virtually every location for any production is in an area free of unsightly masts and signals. For the *Coming Home* crew filming at Porthgwarra Beach there was no hope –

Watched by 13 million viewers, Granada Television Ltd's popular adaptation of Daniel Defoe's classic, Moll Flanders, *contained seventeen sex scenes. Filming at Charlestown took place during a cold snap, so Alex Kingston used bedding of a more modern variety to keep herself warm!*

Filming All the Little Animals. *The sun shone on the camera crew for two weeks while the shot remained resolutely shrouded in mist! (See page 81)*

none of their mobile phones worked – and the lone telephone box earned the nickname 'the office'. Impatient queues, reminiscent of a pre-mobile phone era, formed each day and the coin-box had to be emptied several times during the shoot.

Part of the set dressing for *Twelfth Night* at Prideaux Place involved constructing a Tudor battlemented wall with a huge door in the middle. It was entirely created from plywood, then painted, distressed and dressed for the part. As with the mural, not everything went to plan. This time the weather took control and blew the whole thing down.

Atrocious weather also disrupted the *Coming Home* schedule to the extent that an exterior scene was cancelled altogether and was replaced with an interior pub one at The Logan Rock, Treen, near St Levan. Some of the lifeguards were then drafted as extras and presented to the hair stylist for 1930s haircuts. They can be spotted playing dominoes in the background, occasionally drawing on the 'period' Woodbine cigarettes: the

A beautifully constructed scenic wall for Twelfth Night. *But the glorious sunny day gave way to a night fitter for* The Tempest *and the wall was unceremoniously flattened*

cigarettes were authentic reproductions and apparently brought back memories of the real thing. Not so the art department's own version of a pint of bitter – a coloured liquid masquerading as beer which tasted disgusting.

The pub scene involved David McCallum getting into a skirmish – upturned tables, spilt beer, the usual chaos – and lots of retakes. The beer glasses had to be replenished each time the scene was reshot until finally, unable to stomach the vile concoction any longer, one of the extras refused to comply with the call for drinking action until the real stuff was substituted for the artificial brew. No doubt he was then happy to agree to the director's artistic demands until last orders were called.

For a few weeks during the summer of 1996 north Cornwall played host to two feature films which at times were shot almost back-to-back in the same locations. While the crew for *Amy Foster* were set-building at Port Quin, *Oscar and Lucinda's* group were repainting houses at Boscastle. Director Gillian

A young Oscar being filmed at Boscastle

Armstrong chose the wild, harsh coast of north Cornwall to represent Devon for scenes of Oscar's early life. With Ralph Fiennes and Cate Blanchett taking the lead roles, the movie was filmed at Crackington Haven, Port Isaac, Bossiney, Trebarwith and Morwenstow.

Both films dovetailed their locations, and their respective location managers were kept busy informing local people and holiday makers of arrangements. However, on one occasion the unusual activities of a production's art department nearly caused a mass exodus of tourists who were taking advantage of what Cornwall does best – fabulous scenery, sea and, if you're lucky, sunshine. The crew members appeared on the beach dressed from head to toe in the sort of overalls usually worn by people working with hazardous chemicals. Fortunately, they were just making casts of rocks, but it took some explaining to convince everyone that this wasn't a real emergency.

Putting it all together – from props to stunts

Film and television production is all about inventing reality, convincing us that what we see on the screen – the places and the sequence of actions – is true to life. It's a brilliant piece of deception, led by the imagination and artistic vision of the scriptwriter and director. The quality of the end result depends on the ability of the producer and his or her crew to create and package a drama designed to entertain us either at home or on the big screen. The production process is all about teamwork and involves many different departments pulling together, each one a vital cog in the wheel.

The camera/photography department is led by the director of photography (DOP) who works with the camera operator, focus puller, clapper loader (the one who snaps together the little hinged blackboard with 'Scene 3, Take 35' chalked on it), and maybe a camera assistant or trainee. The creative skills of the DOP influence the overall look of a film. In *Twelfth Night*, for

The low budget film Pigment *being made on the beach at Gwithian Towans, near Hayle*

The crew of Pigment, *perhaps thinking the sea looks inviting!*

instance, Clive Tickner shot through a 'tobacco filter' to 'age it', which gives the film a sepia tint and softens the overall effect. Another traditional trick of the trade came in handy for the *Poldark* camera crew when shooting at St Mawes. They had to find a way to obscure several large tankers which were loitering in the bay. This was accomplished simply by painting period sailing ships onto glass and placing this in front of the camera, thereby making the tankers vanish.

The grip, also part of this unit, is responsible for the various pieces of equipment – dollies, jibs, cherry pickers, etc – required by the camera crew. Specialist grips' equipment is often needed in Cornwall for difficult shots on the edge of cliffs. For *Lighthouse* a helicopter shot off Land's End had to be cancelled due to hurricane-force winds and was replaced at the last minute with one requiring heavy-duty tracking and a jib hired from Bristol.

The only representatives from the sound department seen on location are often the sound recordist, hidden in the background with headphones attached to his or her ears, and a boom operator, holding the long pole with what looks like a giant hairy caterpillar stuck on the end. They're the first to hear that helicopter flying overhead in the middle of a poignant romantic scene.

Whether it's a love letter on parchment paper or a slightly battered Land Rover, the rather archaically named 'property master' with his or her dressing props and standby props must ensure that all those essential items are historically accurate and in the right place at the right time. Sometimes the wrong props just appear from nowhere, as seen in the 1949 version of *Treasure Island*. The sailing vessel *Hispaniola* was supposed to be reaching a remote island, but in the distant background can be seen a reaper and binder cutting corn.

Extras on the set of Amy Foster *at Port Isaac*

Another unwanted prop very nearly ruined one of the closing scenes in *Amy Foster*. The setting is of a horse and cart being driven down the road towards the sea at Port Isaac. This delightful fishing village lends itself perfectly to historical dramas and had been dressed for the part with the aid of a few extra cobbles and some 18th-century props. However, one of the local shopkeepers, perhaps fed up with the influx of a large crew not spending any money, refused to remove an inflatable dinghy hanging outside her shop. The producers decided to solve this problem by purchasing the dinghy, whereupon the shopkeeper, obviously an astute business woman, hung another one outside. An agreement was reached in the end, but not without the intervention of the Cornish Tourist Board, the local vicar and the Parish Council.

In the costume and make-up departments there are several assistants, dressers and wigmakers supporting the designers. The importance of their roles is obvious in lavish costume dramas such as *Twelfth Night* and *Oscar and Lucinda*, but it isn't just the leading ladies whose attire is significant. In *Twelfth Night*, when the pompous servant Malvolio tries to seduce Olivia, a scene touched with humour and pathos so typical of Shakespeare, his yellow, cross-gartered stockings are revealed in all their hideous splendour. The scene was shot in Prideaux Place, with Nigel Hawthorne giving a flawless performance as the ludicrous Malvolio. Incidentally, his toupée, later seen draped on the bald head of Feste (alias Ben Kingsley), was known as Colin.

The lighting director works with the gaffer and best boy. The importance of their role is not always recognised. When we're absorbed by the story line, caught up in the intrigue or riveted to our seats in anticipation of some ghastly horror lurking in the shadows, few of us observe the subtle touches of light that have been deliberately added to enhance the atmosphere.

Lighting came into its own in the dark and sinister interiors

Shooting at Broom Parc near Veryan for The Camomile Lawn, *produced for Channel 4 by Glenn Wilhide and Sophie Balhetcher and directed by Sir Peter Hall*

created at King Arthur's Castle Hotel at Tintagel for *Dracula*, while the skills of the lighting technicians are less obvious in exterior shots of Broom Parc, the house featuring in *The Camomile Lawn*. Broom Parc is a Victorian villa situated on the edge of the cliffs at Camels, near Veryan. The weather refused to co-operate for filming of this Channel 4 production so, with a backdrop of menacing clouds suspended over the sea for the duration of the shoot, an idyllic Cornish summer was created by using arc lights.

The construction crew, including carpenters, painters, plasterers and riggers, build anything from a doorway leading nowhere to a mine shaft for a tricky stunt. Director Beeban Kidron chose Port Quin on the north coast as a key location for her feature film *Amy Foster*. This tiny fishing village belonging to The National Trust consists of little more than a few holiday cottages clustered around the cove. But the director had in mind something more substantial so the crew set to work building a church with churchyard, pub and shop, plus other fishermen's sheds by the water's edge.

Amy Foster was adapted from Joseph Conrad's story about a Ukrainian emigrant, Yanko, played by Vincent Perez, who survives a shipwreck and lands on the shore of a remote fishing village. Beeban Kidron wanted Cornwall for its 'very rugged and changing landscape. It's cold, sunny; it storms, it rages. And then there is the sea. It's the English landscape at its most exotic.' Amy Foster's cottage was built in a wild and isolated location at Pentire Head, perched just above a 90-metre drop. By the time the construction crew had finished the job, it looked as though it had been there for decades. Fortunately, their workmanship was sound enough to withstand a force 12 hammering from Hurricane Lily.

Special effects and stunt experts are brought in for scenes demanding their technical knowledge, equipment and skills.

As well as a cottage on an exposed headland, Amy Foster *required a whole new village at Port Quin*

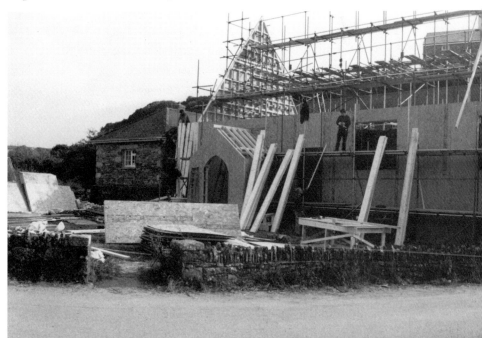

A stunt producer's dream turned into a nightmare. The car should have exploded on impact but didn't. The pyrotechnics man had to climb down and defuse his bomb

They can give us a touch of snow, gloomy fog and devastating fires, people falling off horses, jumping from cars hurtling over cliffs, being propelled from boats, and so on. Weeks, often months, of planning goes into scenes which are phenomenally expensive to produce and potentially dangerous, but which often last just a few seconds on the screen.

However well the production team have prepared for a stunt, it can still go horribly wrong. During the filming of one episode of *Wycliffe*, a car which was supposed to plunge off a cliff and explode succeeded in the first part but failed in the second. The pyrotechnics expert had no choice but to climb under the car, which was still rigged with explosive, and sort things out. In the end the sequence was saved by some clever editing.

For *Amy Foster*, filmed almost entirely on location in Cornwall in 1996, Charlestown harbour was adapted for a crucial storm scene. A crane and 'tip tanks' rocked and rolled one of Square Sail's boats, while wind machines added to the effect. For the interior shots, stuntmen fell out of bunk-beds (but were subsequently edited out!) and the leading actor, Vincent Perez, stylishly vomited... chicken soup (a useful prop).

Jeremy Thomas, director of the thriller *All the Little Animals*, had an ambitious set constructed for a stunt at Wheal Coates. It consisted of a ramp leading to a mine shaft, both positioned to take full advantage of coastal scenery and the sea. The idea was that a Rolls Royce would be driven at high speed down the ramp and would then fall into the mine. Unfortunately, what the producers did not know was that this area of Cornwall is prone to lingering fog, fog that disperses briefly then closes in again, sometimes for days on end. Ideal for *Sherlock Holmes*, perhaps, but a nightmare for this production which had to call for some pretty creative accounting. With stuntman, Rolls Royce and the whole crew on standby, the fog didn't clear for nearly two weeks and, to add to the general sense of powerlessness and frustration, within a few hundred metres of the set the sun beamed relentlessly down from a cloudless sky.

All the Little Animals was made in 1997 and it received a favourable reception when screened at Cannes. It's the story of Bobby, described as a 'simple young man' and played by Christian Bale, who is trying to escape from his stepfather (Daniel Benzali) who in turn is bent on stealing Bobby's inheritance. Bobby takes refuge with an eccentric recluse, Mr Summers (John Hurt).

The majority of location filming for this feature film took place on the Isle of Man, which at the time was offering tempting tax breaks to production companies, but the island could not replicate the spectacular north coast of Cornwall with its mining heritage and precipitous cliffs.

Over the years, with the judicious use of props and set dressing, Cornwall has successfully masqueraded as various foreign lands, thereby allowing producers to save money on transporting their crew abroad. Back in the 1930s, a film originally called *Brown on Resolution*, later renamed *Forever England* and released in the United States as *Born for Glory* was shot in the Falmouth area. It is based on a story by CS Forester, set in the year 1914, and centres around a seaman holding a German warship at bay in the Mediterranean...with a rifle. John Mills and Betty Balfour starred, and it was praised by *Variety* magazine as 'a milestone in British pictures'.

In 1953 director Delmer Davies used Newquay to represent Tallinn in Estonia (then part of the USSR) for *Never Let Me Go*, and for the second series of *Poldark* St Mawes Castle was transformed into Fort Baton in Brittany. Newquay changed identity once more in 1989 to become Brittany again for *Ball Trap at the Côte Sauvage*, a BBC television drama with Jack Shepherd, Zoë Wanamaker and Miranda Richardson. And for Granada's *Moll Flanders*, Turnaware Point on the Roseland Peninsula stood in for the coast of North America.

It's not unusual for directors to decide to split locations if one property does not quite fulfil all their needs. In *Never Let Me Go*, Clark Gable and Gene Tierney escape by car from a theatre. Gable, an American, has fallen in love with Tierney, a Russian ballerina, and they are pursued by Russians towards Newquay harbour. By the time they get to the quay, they are in fact in Mevagissey, and it's here the car veers off the edge into the sea.

In the original series of *Poldark*, Botallack Manor Farm was used to represent the front of Nampara, while Pendeen Manor took over for the back. Again in *Twelfth Night*, seamless editing of two buildings gives the appearance of one. Olivia's house is actually a combination of Prideaux Place and Lanhydrock, and for several of the key scenes between her and Cesario/Viola

(Imogen Stubbs) a specially constructed gateway (the one that blew down), carefully aged to blend in with Prideaux Place, opened in one garden and closed in another more than a few miles distant.

Sometimes, despite all that Cornwall has to offer the film maker, the county just cannot compete against budgetary constraints. Cornish locations are dropped in favour of studio sets and other locations nearer to crew bases, production facilities and post-production houses. This is precisely what happened with an HTV drama series, *Forgotten Story*, over forty years ago.

Forgotten Story was based on a Winston Graham tale and starred an American actor called Val Johnson. With shooting to take place in Cornwall, the production buyer, Bryn Siddall, worked for three weeks getting props organised. In particular he needed period – 1890s – clinker-built boats, including several that had to look really dilapidated, if not wrecked. Not only did he find suppliers for many suitable boats, he also found a farm with an incredible collection of horse-drawn vehicles in various states of disrepair – just what he wanted.

After all this effort, the co-producers pulled out and the whole production was shifted north to the Bristol area. A waterside inn set was built in the studios and, with the addition of a few strands of seaweed, Castle Combe in Wiltshire was converted into a Cornish fishing village, although rumour has it there were problems with trout jumping in the stream. Some of the boats were transported on low loaders to an airfield near Bath where they were then placed on tyres and rocked about to give the impression of rough seas. Various film archives were raided for 'authentic' shots of the sea. Buckets of water were also enthusiastically thrown over the actors and a fire hose brought in to give the impression of stormy weather. The finished product was pure fictional Cornwall.

Very occasionally productions are filmed at the original writer's intended location. In 1953 someone came up with the brilliant idea of filming *The Knights of the Round Table* at Tintagel. It was one of the few films that could be shot at a historically related location. Ava Gardner was Guinevere, Robert Taylor Lancelot, and support came from Stanley Baxter.

MGM started right on target with this Cornish legend filmed in a Cornish location using the very walls of Arthur's supposed seat. Well, at least they began with good intentions. If you happen to see the picture, try to ignore the fact that Camelot looks a little like a castle built around the rocks of Haytor on Dartmoor. Yet again the scenery changes from Cornwall to Devon and back again, the result, according to the critics, being a disappointingly flat film. Judging from our records this is the only time the story of Arthur has been shot in Cornwall.

Stunts are expensive. This ramp was specially constructed for All the Little Animals *so that a Rolls Royce could apparently plunge down it into a mine shaft – but in such a way that the car wouldn't be a write-off!*

Extras queuing for their lunch. It's not the earning that counts, it's the taking a part!

The unsung heroes

Cornwall boasts several large country estates which have proved invaluable to location managers seeking to film away from prying eyes and unpredictable visitors. Boconnoc, Trewithen, Port Eliot and Tregothnan are just a few. Of course a vast amount of land is owned by the Duchy of Cornwall. Often the estate workers are recruited to help in some capacity or are enrolled as extras, but occasionally there is a breakdown in communication and the result can be a bit of a shock.

After the gamekeeper on the Trewithen Estate had finished feeding the pheasants one day, he returned to the estate office following his normal route through the garden of Golden Manor. No doubt there are ghostly anecdotes associated with this gracious Elizabethan house, but the last thing he expected to see was a coffin being carried by pall bearers and accompanied by a sombre group of mourners all dressed in Elizabethan costume. Apparently, he stumbled into the office, white as a

The Headland Hotel,
Newquay, location for
The Witches

sheet, only to be informed that it was part of a German production company's shoot.

For the staff at another location, The Headland Hotel, Newquay, the drama was not confined to filming. In *The Witches,* a feature length adaptation of Roald Dahl's story, The Headland was acting as the venue for a witches' convention. Led by Anjelika Huston, the witches were planning to turn all the world's children into mice. One of the principal actors had retired to his room for a well-earned rest when someone noticed water seeping through the ceiling and cascading down the stairs. Tracing the source of the stream to his room, the manager cautiously knocked on the door, only to be greeted with, 'Go away! I'm asleep!' It took some persistence to rouse the poor man and persuade him that this was an emergency. Exhausted by the rigours of acting, he'd put the plug in his bath, turned on the taps, and fallen asleep.

It is remarkable how Cornwall adapts to the needs of both tourists and film makers who bring money into a county that is struggling to survive economically while facing the depletion of fish stocks, agricultural depression and the uncertain future of its last tin mine. There are relatively few complaints about productions on location; more often than not, visitors find the whole process quite fascinating. It brings excitement and sometimes glamour to their holidays, something to be remembered long after they've removed the sand from their cars.

One lady, Mary Priddey, who now lives in Totnes, Devon, wrote a daily account of her holiday in Tintagel for two weeks in June 1953. She recalls, 'At first we were mystified seeing so many figures clothed in medieval suits of armour walking through the main street and assumed it was some sort of pageant. They looked most incongruous mixing with holiday makers and window shopping...' All was later revealed to Mrs Priddey when she found out that MGM were filming *The Knights of the Round Table*. She watched battle scenes being re-enacted close to Tintagel Castle and remembered how visitors and local people were allowed to walk on the sets when they weren't filming to inspect the 'mock ups' and 'dead bodies' lying face down with arrows in their backs.

As with so many productions made in Cornwall, *The Knights of the Round Table* benefited from the support and active participation of nearby residents. During the battle scenes at Tintagel, the fire brigade were continually on set to extinguish fires caused by the burning arrows.

To their cost, many film crews have little respect for local knowledge which could be so useful to them, particularly when it comes to the vagaries of the weather, and the movement of the tides and currents. It may be that global warming is changing weather patterns, but for concise, short-term predictions the indigenous population win hands down over the 'experts'. Mary Priddey recalled the comment of an elderly man standing next to her watching the MGM shoot. It was an overcast day and a reflector was being used to try to cast light on the actor's face for a close-up shot. He said, 'They won't get no luck till the moon changes next week.' Sure enough, the following week was hot and sunny.

Contrary to some press reports, film makers are generally welcomed by local people and businesses in Cornwall, especially if they are shooting in the winter when many coastal areas of

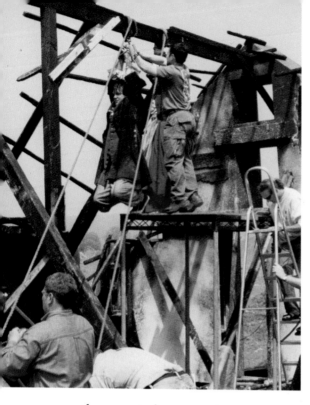

Any extra will tell you the job involves a lot of hanging about, but for Frenchman's Creek this was literally the case. Extras were required to hang, apparently by the neck, from the roof-beam of a ransacked and burnt building

the county become ghost towns – no tourists, empty holiday cottages, hotels closed. The tourist trade provides seasonal, usually poorly paid, work for a few people; television and film production also supplies sporadic work but, especially for extras, it can be a helpful way to supplement their income and add a touch of the old Cornish spirit to the silver screen.

Hotels, guest houses and B&Bs benefit by accommodating cast and crew. Local businesses may be asked to supply anything from Cornish palms to construction materials, from wet suits to mobile toilets. Occasionally, when scenes are being filmed with many extras, local caterers are called in, and sometimes other people may be recruited, such as drivers, security guards, runners and stand-by carpenters. And, with so much shooting of the ocean, all kinds of sea vessels are used: anything from a fully equipped motor boat for safety cover to a gaff-rigged schooner for a period production.

The vessel's skipper, and others who have spent their lives on or around boats, are then cajoled into dressing in costume and appearing as extras. When three fishermen from Newquay, known to their friends as 'Mick the Diver, Spanish and Jimmy', were called upon to row a gig, *The Flippen*, for *Poldark*, they received the princely sum of £26 per day. This was to cover their loss of earnings from fishing. Compare that with the 15 shillings earned by 11-year-old John Corin for being a passenger on a Western National bus in the 1938 film *Yellow Sands*.

Extras are just as versatile as locations: when Newquay took on the identity of a Soviet town for *Never Let Me Go*, the Russian band performing on the dais was in fact Newquay Town Band. By this time (1953) extras were being paid £3 15s a day and for Graham Lane, a youngster in those days, being an extra also meant looking after his prop, a balalaika.

Working as an extra is far from glamorous and invariably involves a great deal of standing around, often for hours on end: while waiting to play their part as a wassailing mob for *The Lord of Misrule*, the extras had to suffer twelve very chilly hours.

Two hundred wet-suited corpses on Port Quin beach

However, there are compensations in the form of readily available food on set, but there is no mollycoddling such as happens to the stars who are given their own personal drivers and private trailer homes.

For historical dramas set before the 20th century, the extras' co-ordinator obviously needs to find people with a certain look – long hair is preferred. So, what better place to start your search than in the surfing haunts of the north coast? Surfers turn up everywhere – as dead Ukrainians in *Amy Foster* and as soldiers in *Frenchman's Creek*. Firing muskets on the harbourside at Charlestown is one thing, but lying around in the water at Port Quin for what must seem like an eternity, even with a wet suit on under the costume, and then being carted off to the graveyard to be certified dead, that is quite another. It really is a dog's, or rather, extra's life!

Lord of Misrule, *Fowey, 1995*

And the rest

We have focused on the world of drama production for our book about filming in Cornwall, but of course hundreds of factual, light entertainment and news programmes have also been shot in the region since television became a reliable medium for conveying information. Cornwall is such a popular destination for holiday makers that every type of holiday programme has visited the county at one time or another to do a feature on tourist attractions and places to stay. TV personalities have walked from one end of the peninsula to the other to expound the virtues of the South West Coast Path, the Camel Trail and hiking on Bodmin Moor.

Cornwall's luxuriant gardens – Trebah, Trelissick, Tresco, Heligan – with their fantastic sub-tropical vegetation have appeared on a whole range of gardening programmes too. A Channel 4 series was devoted entirely to the restoration of The Lost Gardens of Heligan, and later returned to see how they had progressed. The BBC's Natural History Unit comes to Cornwall every now and again to film a rare species of butterfly or the diversity of marine life. A French documentary crew visited the Isles of Scilly in 1998 to shoot a programme on seals.

The so-called Cornish hum (a noise rather like windmills on a wind farm and claimed by some to be heard all the time) was thought to be interesting enough for a documentary by Splash Productions, and ship wrecks, such as *The Hanover*, have been explored with underwater cameras. *Blues and Twos* produced a programme about the Cornwall Air Ambulance and *999* have visited Cornwall on several occasions to reconstruct real-life dramas. One of their recent reconstructions was about three Penlee lifeboatmen who saved a whale trapped close to the shore. They managed to put a rope on it and turn it around to face the open sea.

The Two Fat Ladies – utterly soaked and utterly irrepressible

And then of course there are the cookery programmes led by Rick Stein. (If you're thinking of visiting Padstow, his restaurant is pretty easy to find, but just in case you get lost, ask for 'Padstein'.) One of the most appealing cult culinary programmes to hit our screens is *Two Fat Ladies*, with Jennifer Paterson and Clarissa Dickson Wright bumbling along on their signature motorbike and sidecar. The unfortunate ladies were treated to the most abysmal weather for their shoot at Mevagissey and Hemmick Beach, but they gamely ploughed on, picking mussels to cook on site and looking progressively more bedraggled as rain and fog closed in around them. They didn't complain; after all, this is Cornwall, offering up the fruits of the sea right on cue. It's a place of contrasts, where the elements dictate its mood, and it is certainly never dull.

Films and locations

Year	Production	Cornish location
1929	Street of Abandoned Children	St Ives; Mevagissey
1929	The Manxman	Cornwall
1938	Yellow Sands	Sennen Cove
1940	The Thief of Baghdad	Gunwalloe
1941	Ghost Train	Liskeard Station
1942	Next of Kin	Mevagissey
1944	Love Story	Minack Theatre, Porthcurno
1945	Johnny Frenchman	Mevagissey
1947	Miranda	Polperro, Looe
1948	Scott of the Antarctic	Falmouth Docks
1949	Treasure Island	Carrick Roads, Rivers Fal and Helford, Gull Rock
1951	Circle of Danger	*unknown*
1953	Knights of the Round Table	Tintagel
1953	Never Let Me Go	Mullion Harbour, Newquay, Mevagissey
1957	Dangerous Exile	Porthluney Cove, Carrick Roads, Falmouth Bay/Harbour, Caerhays Castle
1959	Behemoth the Sea Monster	Looe
1963	Crooks in Cloisters	St Mawes
1963	Stolen Hours	Fowey
1967	Magical Mystery Tour	Newquay, Towan Beach, Bodmin
1969	The Bed Sitting Room	St Austell
1971	Straw Dogs	St Buryan, Lamorna Cove
1971	Stocker's Copper	Cornwall
1971	Crucible of Terror	Jericho Valley, Blue Hills
1972	Doomwatch	Polperro, Mevagissey
1970s	Dracula	St Michael's Mount, Carlyon Bay, Mevagissey
1970s	Malachi's Cove	Tintagel, Trebarwith Strand
1970s	Rebecca	Caerhays Castle, Porthluney Cove
1970s	Doctor Who	St Austell clay pits
1970s	Blake's Seven	St Austell clay pits
1972-9	The Onedin Line	Mousehole, Charlestown
1975	Poldark series 1 and 2	Throughout Cornwall

Year	Production	Cornish location
1976	The Eagle Has Landed	Charlestown, RAF St Mawgan, Newquay
1976	The Dame of Sark	Porth Mellin
1978	My Son, My Son	Tremayne Quay, Carwinion, Nare Head
1978	Dracula (Bram Stoker)	Tintagel, St Michael's Mount
1979	Penmarric	Penwith Peninsula, Zennor Head & Cape Cornwall, Botallack, Levant mine, Trengwainton
1980	The Badness within Him (*aka* Last Summer's Child)	Penberth Cove
1980	Priest of Love	Porthzennor Cove
1980	The Onedin Line	Turnaware Point
1981	Nightmare Man	Trebarwith Strand, Port Isaac
1981	The Island of Adventure	Wheal Coates, Mullion Cove, Poldhu Cove
1981	Omen III (The Final Conflict)	St Austell, Luxulyan, Prideaux Place
1982	To the Lighthouse	Carbis Bay, Hayle, Lelant, St Erth - St Ives railway, Bosigran Head
1982	My Cousin Rachel	Gribbin Head, Vault and Lantivet beaches, Boconnoc, Lostwithiel
1982	Jamaica Inn	Port Quin, Polzeath, Pentireglaze Haven
1982	The Flame and The Sword	Bedruthan Steps, Boscastle
1983	Top Secret	Holywell, Godrevy
1983	A Distant Scream	Kynance Cove, Mullion Harbour
1983	Samson and Delilah	Cornish Engines
1984	Robin of Sherwood	Rinsey, St Michael's Mount
1987	Sherlock Holmes, 'Devil's Foot'	Trewardreva Manor
1988	The Return of Sherlock Holmes	Lizard Peninsula, Cadgwith, West Penwith moors, Boskednan
1988	The Wild Things	Newquay
1988	When the Whales Came	Isles of Scilly (Bryher and Samson)
1988	The Witches	Newquay
1989	First and Last	Land's End
1989	The Shell Seekers	St Ives, Lamorna Cove, Porthgwarra, Marazion
1989	Shootout at the OK Tea Rooms	St Just

Year	Production	Cornish location
1989	Ball Trap at the Côte Sauvage	Newquay, Crantock and Fistral beaches, Holywell Bay
1980s	Ripping Yarns – Whinfrey's Last Case	Cape Cornwall
1980s	Charles Darwin – The Voyage of the Beagle	Charlestown
1980s	The Revenge of Billy the Kid	Mousehole
1980s	Jumping the Queue	Looe
1990	The Tale of Little Pig Robinson	Polperro
1991	The Camomile Lawn	Broom Parc, Veryan
1992	Inspector Alleyn	Tintagel, Glebe Cliffs
1993	The Three Musketeers	Charlestown, Boconnoc Estate, Lanhydrock, Pentire, Rumps
1993	Cycle of Death (Wycliffe pilot)	Penzance, Marazion
1994	Blue Juice	Newquay, St Ives, Mousehole, Chapel Porth, Godrevy
1994	The End of Summer The Carousel	Padstow, Bude, Widemouth Bay, Prideaux Place, Ethy House
1994/5	Wycliffe series 1/2	Throughout Cornwall
1995	The Lord of Misrule	Fowey
1995	Bugs	Tamar Estuary
1995	Daisies in December	St Ives, St Michael's Mount
1995	The Empty House; Another View; Voices in Summer; Snow in April	Throughout Cornwall
1995	Poldark – Stranger from the Sea	Rinsey, Lansallos, Coombe Haven, Penrose Estate
1995	The Wind in the Willows	Camel Estuary
1995	Twelfth Night	Lanhydrock, Cotehele, Mt Edgcumbe, Prideaux Place, St Michael's Mount
1995	Treasure Island	Charlestown
1995	The Vet	Bohetherick
1996	Moll Flanders	Charlestown Harbour, River Fal, Turnaware Point
1996	Tea with the Professor	Antony House, Port Eliot
1996	Amy Foster	Throughout Cornwall
1996	Thief Takers	St Ives and the Towans
1996	Jonathan Creek	Rinsey Head

Year	Production	Cornish location
1996	Oscar and Lucinda	Boscastle, Crackington Haven, Bossiney, Trebarwith, Morwenstow
1996	Rebecca	Charlestown
1996	Coming Home	Prideaux Place, Lelant, Godrevy Point, Penzance, Porthgwarra Beach, Marazion
1996	Wycliffe series 3	Throughout Cornwall
1997	All the Little Animals	Wheal Coates, St Agnes
1997	A Respectable Trade	Charlestown
1997	Hollyoaks	Fistral Beach, Newquay
1997	Plunge	Fistral Beach, Newquay, Watergate Bay
1997/8	Wycliffe series 4/5	Throughout Cornwall
1998	Frenchman's Creek	Charlestown, Helston, Padstow, St Clements, Godolphin House
1998	War Zone	Duckpool
1998	Scarlet Pimpernel	Charlestown
1998	The Lighthouse	Longships, Land's End
1998	Mansfield Park	Charlestown
1998	Nancherrow	Chapel Porth, Wheal Coates, Towan Head, Bodmin & Wenford Railway